THE RIGHT CAREER FOR ME

TEACHER

KATHLEEN A. KLATTE

ROSEN PUBLISHING

Published in 2025 by The Rosen Publishing Group, Inc.
2544 Clinton Street, Buffalo, NY 14224

Cover Designer: Michael Flynn
Intertior Designer: Rachel Rising
Editor: Kathleen A. Klatte

Portions of this work were originally authored by Annalise Silivanch and published as *A Career as a Teacher*. All new material in this edition was authored by Kathleen A. Klatte.

Library of Congress Cataloging-in-Publication Data

Names: Klatte, Kathleen A., author.
Title: Teacher / Kathleen A. Klatte.
Description: [Buffalo] : Rosen Publishing, [2025] | Series: The right career for me | Includes index.
Identifiers: LCCN 2024011239 (print) | LCCN 2024011240 (ebook) | ISBN 9781499476408 (library binding) | ISBN 9781499476392 (paperback) | ISBN 9781499476415 (ebook)
Subjects: LCSH: Teaching--Vocational guidance--Juvenile literature.
Classification: LCC LB1775 .K56 2025 (print) | LCC LB1775 (ebook) | DDC 370.71--dc23/eng/20240315
LC record available at
https://lccn.loc.gov/2024011239
LC ebook record available at
https://lccn.loc.gov/2024011240

Manufactured in the United States of America

CPSIA Compliance Information: Batch #CSRYA25. For further information, contact Rosen Publishing at 1-800-237-9932.

CONTENTS

INTRODUCTION

Teaching is an essential career. Wherever you live, you'll find teachers. Of course, most teachers work in schools, but you'll also find them in museums, zoos, and other cultural institutions. Generally, teachers in a school setting teach academic subjects such as math, history, and language arts. However, there are also art and music teachers. In the United States, all children are legally entitled to an appropriate education, so there are also teachers who specialize in working with kids with special needs.

The tools may have changed over time, but the goal of teaching has always been to help students explore and learn about their world.

Everyone remembers special teachers—the ones who inspired and encouraged them.

The best teachers are helpful, interesting people who like to present information in fresh and exciting ways. Many teachers find the career rewarding because they can see some of their impact on students happen before their eyes. It's exciting to see students make connections and grasp concepts. Some students return to visit and talk with their favorite teachers, sharing their successes and asking for advice. Teachers help shape the values, perspectives, and work ethic of the next generation.

Traditionally, teachers work within schools designed for different age groups: preschool, elementary school, middle school, and high school. Each teaching level has its own advantages and challenges. Young children need teachers to help them learn basic academic skills and appropriate school behavior. Middle schoolers—"tweens"—can exhibit a range of maturity levels as they grapple with puberty. Teenagers may require someone to motivate and inspire them. All levels require energy, creativity, and a high level of organization.

Teachers quickly learn that the job requires more than just sharing information. A teacher often must go "above and beyond" to help students achieve. That may mean spending extra time or coaching students through personal problems. Some kids may still be catching up from disrupted learning caused by the COVID-19 pandemic. They also must deal with the new reality of active shooter drills and lockdowns. Today's teachers work in schools that are increasingly diverse, with more students for whom English is a second language. Teacher training now gives teachers strategies to help these students succeed.

Ideas about teaching and learning have changed. Today, successful teachers are good public speakers and instructors, but they also help students take charge of their own learning. This was especially true during the pandemic, when teachers had to figure out ways to teach and keep kids engaged when they weren't even in the same room.

Today's teachers design activities that children can do in an active, hands-on way, such as group explorations, problem-solving exercises, computer-based lessons, or classroom games. Some teachers incorporate music, art, and other creative approaches into their learning material.

Regardless of whether they teach in a school or cultural institution, whether they teach academics or life skills, all teachers educate and inspire the next generation. Keep reading to decide if you have what it takes to be a great teacher.

During the pandemic, teachers had to figure out how to keep kids learning and they had to do it with very little notice.

OTHER PLACES YOU CAN FIND TEACHERS

While most teachers work in schools, there are other places they can find employment. Most major cultural institutions have an education department. They're usually staffed by a combination of professional teachers and volunteers called docents. Teachers at zoos and museums lead tours and teach classes to visitors of all ages. They help develop educational materials for the institution where they work. Often this combines facts about the materials in the collection and the institution itself. Imagine learning all about elephants while standing right in front of one!

The educational staff at the Bronx Zoo teach people about the animals in the collection and the wonderful historic buildings in the park.

CHAPTER ONE

CAREER FACTS

Teaching is a "helping profession." People who are drawn to it have a desire to work directly with people and improve their lives. Teachers love learning and look for new and exciting ways to present information to their students. Presenting lessons in a fresh, original way can sometimes be a challenge when certain things are mandated by federal or local government. So, a person who enjoys a creative challenge can make an excellent teacher. A teacher does much more than simply present information. A teacher thinks on their feet, reacting to and working with the spirit of the students in the room. A good teacher cares whether students learn and feels satisfied when they do.

According to a 2023 survey by *Education Week*, job satisfaction among teachers is on the rise. This follows a historic low in 2022, as teachers and students continue to recover from the disruptions of the pandemic.

A STABLE CAREER

Traditionally, teaching has been seen as a stable job. According to a survey conducted in 2023, the average teaching career is about 15 years. Most teachers stay at the same school for about eight years.

People choose teaching as a profession because they want to help and inspire young minds.

While schools are not immune to economic downturns, public schools with many students don't close overnight. They're supported by taxpayer dollars. If a town's school board decides to make big changes to the school budget, taxpayers usually have the opportunity to approve it or reject it. Teachers usually get plenty of notice about changes, such as in the spring of the previous school year. Further, public schools guarantee a level of security for teachers and administrators who have shown themselves to be capable. After several years of working successfully in a school district, a teacher can be eligible for tenure, or protection from suddenly being fired. Private schools and charter schools are subject to different rules and may offer less job security. In particular, Catholic schools have been closing due to rising tuition and falling enrollment.

The Bureau of Labor Statistics (BLS) predicts only about a 1 percent growth in K-12 teaching jobs over the next decade. However, there will still be thousands of jobs available each year as teachers retire or move on to careers outside the classroom

SALARY AND BENEFITS

According to the BLS, the median salary for K-12 teachers in 2022 was about $60,000, with high school teachers earning slightly more than elementary and middle school teachers. A teacher's salary usually depends on the state's cost of living, or how much it costs to pay for housing and other basic needs. Where it costs more to live, teachers typically get a boost in income. For example, New York City pays the highest average salary at about $90,000 while teachers in Mississippi earn about $47,000. In March 2023, Senator Bernie Sanders introduced the Pay Teachers Act. This is legislation designed to raise the salary of all teachers to at least $60,000.

A teacher's salary also depends on years of experience in the classroom. Most public school districts have a set salary scale. Teachers with the same number of years of work experience are typically paid the same amount. However, extra academic credentials can boost a teacher's salary. A teacher with a master's or doctoral degree, or with multiple certifications, can see increased pay. In general, public school teachers earn about 30 percent more than private school teachers. They've also more likely to belong to a union.

Nearly 70 percent of all public school teachers in the United States belong to a union or other association. A union is a work association that bargains for a salary and benefits such as health insurance and pensions for its members. Unions also bargain for limits to work hours and days and push for better working conditions in schools. The National Education Association (NEA) is the largest teachers' union in the United States. It's also the largest labor union in the country.

Above a standard salary, teachers have multiple ways they can earn extra money. Some are paid to coach extracurricular sports teams or work with an after-school club. They might help with production of the school play or work as part of a school-based tutoring club. Teachers might serve as summer school instructors or have a summer job. Many teachers develop a side career they can pursue during weekends, summers, and other school breaks.

For information on current teachers' salaries, refer to the Bureau of Labor Statistics' Occupational Outlook Handbook (www.bls.gov/oco) or the website of the National Education Association (www.nea.org).

DIFFERENT GRADE LEVELS

Teachers have different job descriptions, depending on the grade level they teach. To help them understand this, they take classes in how children develop. This helps them present material in a way children can understand. In early education classes, teachers act more as guides while children adjust to the social rules of school. Elementary teachers help students develop basic skills in reading, writing, and mathematics. In middle school, teachers help students focus on learning while peer pressure rises around them, and their bodies undergo rapid and drastic changes. In high school, students are starting to discover and develop their talents, and an encouraging teacher can help them do this. A teacher's own education, experiences, and personality may help define what age group and subject matter they would prefer to teach.

EARLY EDUCATION

In today's economy, all the adults in a household generally hold jobs outside the home. Early childhood education programs are important to help children become socialized, prepare them for their academic careers, and to provide supervision while parents are working.

Early education teachers work with the youngest students—preschool and kindergarten. They usually have their own classrooms and work with the same group of students for the entire year. Teachers work hard to design their classrooms with young students in mind. The classroom will usually have areas for different activities: a play area, a quiet reading area, a "circle" area (where students can sit as a group for a lesson or song), and an area of desks or tables for academic work or art.

At the preschool level, a typical day is structured in small sections of time (sometimes only 15 minutes) with activities that change often. Education at this level is more social than academic:

students practice taking turns, raising their hands to speak, and working together. Experts advise that class sizes should be small, with a high teacher-to-student ratio. Students also work on skills in preparation for elementary academics. For example, children develop motor skills through painting or sand play. Early language skills are taught through stories, games, and songs. Introductory math and science skills are involved in counting, building, and nature exploration. Dance, music, and all kinds of art are often used to stimulate young learners. Pre-K programs for four-year-old children are often offered in public school districts. Programs for younger students may be private or community based. A lot depends on the size and resources of the local public school system, although many now recognize the need for early childhood programs.

Generally, children are considered eligible for kindergarten the year they turn 5. This allows them to have developed the motor skills necessary to function somewhat independently in a school setting. In the past, kindergarten classes were play-based, half-day programs that were similar to preschool. However, that has changed in the last few decades. Concerns about children's academic readiness and the need for parents to work have caused schools to develop more academic, full-day programs. Most school districts house kindergarten programs within their elementary schools. Kindergarten teachers now instruct children in phonics (connecting letters to sounds) and early math (recognizing patterns, counting, and doing simple addition). The kindergarten curriculum also includes music, social studies, science, and even computers. In a full-day

An ideal preschool classroom has no more than 16 children and at least two educators.

kindergarten classroom, teachers plan a day that allows for the natural rhythms of snacks, lunch, and rest time along with lessons and activities.

More than ever, children are enrolled in early education programs. School districts are concerned about students' reading levels and standardized test scores. Many districts are expanding their early education programs, especially programs tailored to kids with special needs. Early education seems to prepare children for reading and math earlier. These programs should continue to grow as long as local and state education boards can fund them.

ELEMENTARY SCHOOL

After the shift to academic work in kindergarten, the elementary school teacher's instructional role in the classroom expands. Actual teaching time increases as children's attention spans do, and the subject matter becomes more complex. In grades one through three, a major focus is learning to read. From grade four on, the focus shifts to reading to learn.

Most classroom teachers in first through sixth grade teach multiple basic academic subjects—including math, reading, writing, and social studies—to the same group of students. The children typically have additional teachers for music, art, library/media, computer science, and physical education. Some schools also offer foreign languages. Others have separate teachers for math and science, even at the elementary level. Some districts have moved sixth graders up to middle school to join seventh and eighth graders, while other school districts have found success by instructing sixth and ninth graders in their own schools.

Elementary school teachers, such as early education teachers, may find it rewarding to spend a whole year watching the same group of students grow and learn. They may find one year's class—with all its individual personalities—to be entirely different from last year's. Elementary teachers strive to meet the academic needs of all the children in the class, including higher- and lower-achieving students. This may mean finding time to lead several reading and math groups working at different levels or working with kids who have Individual Education Plans (IEPs). The amount of time invested in encouraging

One of the functions of early education programs is to accustom kids to proper classroom behavior. That way, when they start first grade, the teacher can concentrate on teaching academic material.

children can forge a lasting bond, with many students returning to hug their favorite former teacher.

Generally, kids learn best in an orderly, structured environment. With that in mind, teachers at this level try to establish classroom rules and habits right away, setting the tone for the rest of the year. When they do, students are clear about what rewards they may receive for cooperation and what penalties are given for bad behavior.

AN INTERVIEW WITH PATTY BARRETT TAYLOR, ELEMENTARY SCHOOL TEACHER

How long have you been teaching?
"I have been teaching for 26 years."

When did you know you wanted to be a teacher?
"I think I always wanted to be a teacher. I remember 'playing school' ALL the time as a little kid."

What grades or subjects have you taught?
"I have taught second grade, third grade, Reading Recovery and spent one year as literacy coach (which means that I helped teachers learn more about reading)."

What's your favorite part of being a teacher?
"My favorite part of being a teacher is getting children excited about learning something new and watching them grow confident as a learner."

What's the most challenging aspect of your career?
"The most challenging part of teaching is having certain things that I must teach and not always having time to teach about topics that the children would truly enjoy."

Although the curriculum has advanced since the days of the "three Rs," reading will always be at the heart of elementary education.

MIDDLE SCHOOL AND HIGH SCHOOL

In middle school and high school, most teachers specialize in teaching one academic subject, such as history, English, or Spanish, to many different classes. Teachers need to complete sufficient course work, such as a college major, in the subject they teach. They must also take education courses in which they learn methods for teaching the subject. Some states require teachers to earn a master's degree once they've been hired. Each subject teacher might also have a homeroom class, or a group of students who begin or end the day in the class, for attendance, announcements, and other guidance.

In high school, music (vocal and instrumental) and art classes are often part of a student's week. Also, students typically find many extracurricular clubs, sports teams, and performing arts groups to join after school. Teachers who are paid to lead these groups usually enjoy the chance to work with students outside the classroom and share their expertise in an area of interest.

In addition to more advanced academic work, middle school and high school teachers must deal with youngsters undergoing puberty. Some youngsters mature physically first while others mature behaviorally. They may push boundaries with authority and begin to experience peer pressure to conform to certain fashions or other "in" behavior. Teens and preteens may also start to question their sexuality or their family's religious beliefs.

High school teachers are specialists in their subject. For instance, besides studying a language in school, a foreign language teacher might have participated in an exchange program. They might also spend their vacations visiting places where the language they teach is spoken.

SPECIAL SUBJECTS

In addition to the standard academic subjects, school curriculums also include art, music, physical education, and sometimes vocational classes. These classes require teachers who are specialists in their subject and are trained to teach.

Special subject teachers help students learn in different, but no less valuable, ways than regular classroom teachers do. Special subject teachers can play an important role in a student's education. A child who has a hard time focusing in reading lessons may be the same child who comes to life in a music class. Another child who gets discouraged by math might be a gifted athlete in gym. As for the teachers, they often enjoy the variety that comes from working with children in many different age groups. They may also work with some of the same students from year to year. Special subject teachers may work in one school or travel to several different schools, depending on the resources of the school district where they work. They may be involved in extracurricular activities, aside from their classes. The gym teacher might coach one or more sports teams. The music teacher might direct the holiday concert or be in charge of the band.

SPECIAL EDUCATION

Public school districts in the United States are required by federal law to provide free, appropriate education for all students. This includes children with both physical and intellectual challenges. The Americans with Disabilities Act (ADA) requires all public buildings to be accessible to disabled people. The Individuals with Disabilities Education Act (IDEA) is the latest iteration of laws designed to provide every child with a suitable free education.

Playing in the school band helps students learn how to work together as a group. Music teachers might be assigned to lead extracurricular activities such as marching band.

Special education teachers play a unique role in a school. They serve students with learning disabilities, physical disabilities, and other special needs. They may be part of a team that includes occupational therapists, speech therapists, or social workers. Working with children whose disabilities range from mild to severe, special education teachers bring extra training to their jobs. The students they work with may have a variety of learning or emotional issues. Students may have learning disabilities such as dyslexia, hearing or speech disabilities, emotional disturbances, or autism, just to name a few. Teachers who work with these students use special teaching methods and techniques to help them learn. Because of the demands of this job, many states require special education teachers to have a master's degree in the field.

Teaching jobs in special education are growing at a faster rate than regular teaching jobs. This rise comes as more children are screened for disabilities earlier in life to get them the help they need. In the past, students often went undiagnosed unless they were causing a disturbance. They might have been dismissed as being "shy" or "odd." Evidence has shown that children whose learning difficulties are identified and addressed early have more success in school and in the future. Many school districts are expanding their preschool services to include more programs for special needs children. In addition, federal laws require that students who need special services in school receive them. In many areas of the country, there is a shortage of teachers who are trained in special education. As a result, teachers with the required training are in high demand.

SUBSTITUTE TEACHING

In most jobs, when someone calls out, it's not a big deal. The manager may have to shift someone to cover lunches, but the staff on hand usually just works around the absence. However, when a teacher is ill or has an emergency, it's not possible to leave a room full of children unattended for the day.

To solve this problem, school districts reply upon a roster of substitute teachers. Substitutes usually work "on call" at one or more schools and grade levels and can be called the very morning they are needed. They may be hired to cover longer teacher absences as well, such as when a teacher goes on maternity leave. Substitute teachers are paid only for the days they work, so there is no regular, dependable salary. In addition, substitutes can often be the teachers that students like to pick on, since they believe they can get away with it. The absent teacher may or may not leave a lesson plan for the day. A substitute needs to be resourceful and think on his or her feet to create fun and educationally relevant activities.

Substitute teachers come from all backgrounds: a semiretired individual who enjoys the school environment, a parent returning to work part-time, or a college graduate who is seeking a job in that school district. Substituting is a great way to share an enthusiasm for learning and people. During the COVID-19 pandemic, substitute teachers were in extremely high demand to cover absences and quarantines.

A teacher who's expecting will prepare for when they go on maternity leave. They may even get to meet their substitute ahead of time. Substitute teachers who respond to calls the morning they're needed develop skills for responding to whatever surprises come their way.

CHAPTER TWO

A DAY IN THE CLASSROOM

One of the most gratifying parts of being a teacher is watching a group of children learn and develop new skills throughout the course of the school year. Youngsters may be experiencing a new topic for the first time, or they may suddenly grasp a concept that's eluded them before.

"There's nothing more rewarding than teaching kindergarten," says teacher Kathy Fitzpatrick. "Imagine a child who can barely grasp a pencil entering your classroom in September. Then imagine that same child leaving your classroom in June, writing stories."

When teaching older children, a teacher can help students discover and develop their unique talents. These changes can occur over a series of regular school days, weeks, and months. Teachers must balance the required curriculum for their district and also address current affairs. For example, a presidential election or a space launch are certainly pertinent teaching topics. So how do teachers divide up a school day of six or more hours to help students reach important goals?

Over time, teachers learn what kind of classroom set up works best for them and their students. It might be orderly rows of desks, or several pushed together to make larger units.

AN ELEMENTARY SCHOOL DAY

Children generally learn best in a structured environment, so each elementary school day is organized with time for academics, lunch, recess, snack breaks, and special classes, such as art and gym. An elementary school teacher prepares ahead of time by planning what content the day's lessons will cover and devising related activities. This preparation also includes finding or creating books, worksheets, visual displays, and other materials for each lesson.

Math and language study take up the most teaching time, especially because these two areas make up annual standardized tests. Students in grades three to eight are required to take standardized tests in math and English language arts every year. In some places, the teacher's own assessment is based on their students' scores.

During the day, students spend time as a group learning with the teacher as well as time doing independent work. As students complete assignments, the teacher monitors their progress

Standardized tests are part of a federal initiative to ensure children are learning the skills they need.

and helps children individually as needed. Teachers may also allow students free time in the classroom to explore learning centers or read independently. During some periods, teachers may divide the class into smaller groups based on students' skill levels in a subject, particularly reading. Then they lead lessons geared to the needs of each group.

The day's lessons also include some science, geography, and history, or all of these combined in some way. As an example, a class study of ancient Egypt can include nearly every subject and some hands-on craft projects. Such a unit can reach students of all different learning styles.

As students leave the classroom for lunch or other classes, a teacher may have some time for lesson preparation, grading, or communication with parents. Or they may be scheduled to supervise children in the cafeteria or on the playground. The normal flow of the day might be interrupted for an assembly or special event or for an emergency drill.

Near the end of the school day, teachers spend time explaining homework assignments to the students. They make sure the children understand what they need to bring home to complete their work. Once students are dismissed for the day, the teacher still has lots of work ahead: grading, preparing worksheets and reading materials for the next day, making notes about students' behavior and progress, and cleaning up the classroom. They might have to supervise detention or an extracurricular activity. A school may also schedule after-school meetings or professional development (extra training for teachers) with faculty and supervisors. This can make for a long day. Many teachers don't leave until 5 p.m. after arriving at school by 7:30 a.m. or earlier.

Teachers are usually working throughout the day—even when they're supposed to be at lunch.

STANDARDIZED TESTING

Standardized tests have been around since the 1960s. The purpose of these tests is to ensure that all children in the same grade are achieving the same academic milestones. The tests are administered nationwide and scored by computer, removing any local bias from the grading process.

The Every Student Succeeds Act (2015) requires annual standardized testing in math and language arts for grades three through eight, plus testing in science certain years. Some people feel there is too much emphasis placed on these tests. Teachers must spend time teaching the material covered in the tests, as well as test prep so kids understand how to take the test. This takes time that could be used to teach a more varied curriculum, including things such as visiting art museums, or learning about local history.

In addition, some students become very anxious about taking formal proctored tests. Of course, older teens will need to take this sort of test eventually, but people worry it's too stressful for younger kids. There is concern that children who are too nervous about taking the tests will freeze up and not score as well as they could.

In some places, teachers' own annual assessments are based on how well their students score on the tests. This adds pressure to teachers and students alike. Some people worry this emphasis on tests is creating a generation of children who know how to be test takers instead of how to be creative thinkers.

A MIDDLE SCHOOL OR HIGH SCHOOL DAY

Teachers at the middle and high school levels interact with more students for a smaller amount of time. Depending on the size of the school, they might teach the same subject to multiple grade levels, or they might specialize in honors or advanced placement (AP) classes. The school day is broken up into units of instruction that might last for one or two periods. As a result, teachers need to get in and out of lessons quickly and smoothly and build the subject a little each day. Concepts are explored in more depth at this level, and teachers create more tests and writing assignments to measure students' progress. Because secondary teachers are trained extensively in their subjects, they are expected to be good sources of information. For example, foreign language teachers might vacation in places where the language they teach is spoken, so they're knowledgeable about the country and its culture.

The schedules of middle and high schools tend to build in more breaks for teachers. Some schools give teachers a prep period during the day devoted to grading, lecture preparation, and other tasks. When they don't have a regular class, a teacher may be assigned to monitor a study hall or cafeteria. Many teachers also have a homeroom. In addition, they may lead an extracurricular activity. Foreign language teachers might lead a club or chaperone student trips. English teachers might supervise the yearbook or school newspaper.

SUMMERS OFF?

When discussing a career as a teacher, many people cite the perk of summers off. Most teachers in the United States receive the traditional two-month break after a ten-month school year. While some people consider such a schedule to be a luxury, many teachers believe it is a necessity to take a break from the intensity of school. This is particularly true now that lockdowns and active shooter drills are part of school. In addition, teachers are coping with deficits caused by quarantines during the pandemic, and the resurgence of assorted viruses and "bugs" now that students are attending in-person classes full time again. Philadelphia-area teacher Anna Weiss, writing for the Philadelphia Public School Notebook, points out that the summer break may be the only way some teachers avoid career burnout.

Summer school isn't always a punishment for failing a class. Some students take classes over the summer to get ahead on their college requirements.

"I personally work about 60 to 70 hours a week," she says. "It's more than I'm contracted to work, but I willingly do it because in teaching, it's just a given that you're going to work outside of the school day."

But how many teachers really have the whole summer "off?" After the last day of class, teachers still must pack up their classrooms. Some materials may need to be returned to central storage areas. The room may need to be left in a certain condition to accommodate deep cleaning or repairs. And of course, there's always paperwork!

Some teachers do opt to spend their summer with their family or traveling for leisure. However, many teachers work a second job to bring in additional income. They may work as tutors, summer-session instructors, or camp counselors. Some teachers may spend some of their summer chaperoning student trips. Others use the time to do professional development, attending summer courses or conferences that will help them improve their teaching. They may also work to complete an additional degree.

At the end of summer, teachers return to the classroom before students. They need to set up and decorate their rooms and meet with the rest of the staff to plan the year. In some places, they may need to submit lesson plans for approval before classes resume.

However, the traditional teaching schedule may be changing. Some schools have shifted to (or will shift to) a year-round schedule with regular breaks. This is referred to as a balanced calendar. This new schedule is more common in the southern

Some people think a year-round school schedule such as many Asian nations use would prepare kids better for success in a global workplace

and western states. Educators have found that the constant structure prevents "summer learning loss" and removes some of the risks to children that an unstructured summer might bring, especially in areas where parents might not be able to afford to send their children to summer camp. More frequent breaks also seem to help prevent burnout in students and teachers. The balanced calendar breaks up the school year into more even segments than the current system. Currently, 25 states allow a year-round school schedule.

One of the main concerns of a year-round schedule is the need for working parents to find childcare during vacations or "intercessions" that occur at odd times of the year. Most camp programs are structured to operate between Memorial Day and Labor Day. Proponents of the year-round schedule suggest that schools might offer enrichment programs to keep children safely occupied during breaks.

CHRISTA MCAULIFFE

Christa McAuliffe (1948–1986) was a high school teacher from New Hampshire. NASA selected her out of 11,000 applicants to be the first teacher—in fact the first civilian of any kind—to fly in space. She trained for months at the Johnson Space Center in Houston, Texas, to prepare for her mission aboard the space shuttle Challenger. She had to learn how to function in zero gravity and live in the confines of the space shuttle just like any other astronaut. She planned to teach science lessons aboard the shuttle which would be broadcast back on Earth.

On January 28, 1986, people gathered at Cape Canaveral in Florida and in front of televisions across the country to watch the launch. Tragically, the shuttle exploded two minutes after launch, resulting in the deaths of the entire crew.

McAuliffe's pioneering spirit is honored and remembered today with an educational center at Framingham State College and a planetarium in Concord, New Hampshire, that bear her name. During the 2017–2018 school year, astronauts aboard the International Space Station completed the lessons she planned to teach in space.

Christa McAuliffe (female astronaut on the left) underwent rigorous training to prepare for her time in space.

CHAPTER THREE

WHAT DOES IT TAKE TO BE A GOOD TEACHER?

People have long known that a good teacher can have a lifelong impact on students. Many people have fond memories of that special teacher who inspired them to try something new or to excel when they were discouraged. However, a recent study has been able to quantify some amazing facts.

- A good teacher can impact the lives of as many as 3,000 students.
- Eighty-three percent of students say a teacher helped raise their self-esteem and confidence.
- A good teacher is more likely to inspire students to go on to college and a well-paying career, boosting their lifetime income by thousands of dollars.

But what makes someone a good candidate for a teaching career? Academic knowledge and the methodology of teaching can be learned, but good teachers also need certain personality traits.

PERSONALITY

The BLS considers the following qualities important for prospective teachers:

- patience
- resourcefulness
- physical stamina
- excellent communication and organizational skills

Although there's an enormous amount of focus on standardized tests, a teacher with passion and creativity can still make the classroom come alive with ideas, discussion, and engaging activities. The qualities of patience and cooperation create a peaceful place for conflict-free learning. Organization is key for planning lessons, grading papers, and working with multiple IEPs. Finally, teachers may need authority most of all because if students don't respect a teacher's guidelines, no learning can take place.

Energy and enthusiasm are important: a teacher needs to find a way to motivate students who may be tired, distracted, or discouraged. They also need to be adaptable. Classrooms may include students who are neurodivergent or speak English as a second language.

Different grade levels require different personalities, or at least an ability to change one's approach. Preschool and kindergarten students feel safe in an unfamiliar environment if their teacher is understanding and caring. These youngest students are still learning social and life skills. Fifth graders

A good teacher inspires students to achieve excellence, both individually and as a group.

appreciate a little wackiness from a creative teacher since they are beginning to plug into their own talents and confidence. Middle and high school students will admire a teacher who leads the class with respectful authority, but also brings humor into the classroom.

SKILLS

Being a "people person" is a helpful trait for a career that involves a great deal of public speaking, as well as other forms of communication. A teacher-in-training develops and practices the specific teaching skills needed in the classroom. An effective teacher must plan a course of study appropriate to an age group and then manage the class's attention and interest. A teacher evaluates each student's understanding of concepts and his or her social and emotional functioning in the classroom. They'll learn how to gauge which students can be given a measure of leeway and which ones require more discipline. Finally, a teacher needs to get along with and share ideas with other teachers, as well as communicate with parents and welcome their questions. Over time, teachers learn the best ways to approach the challenges in each area.

CLASSROOM MANAGEMENT

Keeping a classroom of students focused is no small job. Each child brings their own feelings and energy levels to the group. Children are affected by whatever is going on at home. If their home life is unsettled, they may be tired, hungry, stressed, or even angry. Or an impending holiday may have them restless and excited. For whatever reason, they may be resisting the very idea of being in school that day.

Being polite and taking turns helps a classroom run well.

To bring a level of focus, teachers need to create a clear structure in a classroom. In elementary school, teachers give a certain rhythm to the day. They do this by setting up a daily schedule to help the classroom run smoothly. These routines help students get involved in each learning activity and behave appropriately. Routines also help signal the beginning and end of each activity. They can also help children learn to focus—if they know that they'll be allowed to get up for recess or lunch at a certain time they can sit still through the lesson. In older grades, this structure becomes more academic in nature. For example, there may be a certain pace to projects and a certain day each week for quizzes. This sort of structure helps students learn to manage their own time.

Children, like adults, work best when there is a goal. As a result, many successful teachers use incentives, or rewards, to keep students focused. Kindergarten and early elementary students might be rewarded with daily stars on a chart; some teachers allow them to choose a small prize when they have a certain number of stars. Young children are also happy when they get back a successful test or assignment with a colorful sticker. Older students respond to different incentives. They might enjoy a movie at the end of a productive week or earn a pass to have a homework assignment eliminated.

A classroom's physical space also helps shape how children learn. This is especially important in the early grades. Teachers create visual displays and stations around the room that help physically and mentally organize children. Art supplies might be stored in one part of the room and student projects might be displayed elsewhere. An elementary school classroom often includes a large calendar, world map, a display of the alphabet and possibly one for multiplication tables or counting. The room might include a lending library for the class. For younger children, the teacher may also post the day's weather; older students might see notes telling when projects are due. Bulletin boards with student work and photographs can help each child feel that he or she is a meaningful part of the class. Holiday displays can guide students toward what's next, both seasonally and in their work.

Creating lesson plans takes time and organization. Many people don't understand how much teachers work outside the school to make sure their classroom runs smoothly.

PLANNING FOR SUCCESS

Common Core is a set of standards used by many states to ensure that all students meet the same educational milestones. However, students in each grade have always been expected to learn certain concepts and skills by the end of the school year. The teacher's task is to break that material down into manageable sections they can teach, and students can demonstrate that they've mastered the information.

To accomplish this, a teacher creates units of study within each subject area. For example, a teacher may create a unit on plants for earth science or a unit on multiplication for math. Each unit contains a series of lesson plans. A lesson plan is a description of a specific lesson. It explains what students will learn that day and how it will be presented to them. Teacher training programs include lesson plan development, and student teaching assignments allow lesson plans to be tested with children.

A well-developed lesson plan includes the title of the lesson, the time needed to complete it, and the materials required. It also states the lesson's objective, or what the student will do or know by the end. Within the plan, the teacher outlines how the lesson will progress. An innovative plan brings different skills together—science and writing, for example. Depending on the teacher's goals for the lesson, the plan may center on a group activity or individual learning. Finally, the plan explains how students will be evaluated. For example, the teacher may look at student work from the lesson to determine what students have learned and what they still need to master. This part of the teaching process is called assessment. After the lesson is completed with students, the teacher notes its successes and failures and how to improve it. In addition, the lesson plan needs to be flexible enough to accommodate different learning styles and abilities within the class.

Depending on a school's procedures, the principal may require each teacher to submit lesson plans in advance on a regular basis, such as weekly. Other principals may be more informal and may just want to know that lesson plans are being prepared. There has been controversy recently because some states have introduced bills that would require teachers to submit an entire year's worth of lesson plans before the school year begins. Many people feel this isn't feasible. Planning so far in advance doesn't leave flexibility to accommodate students' different learning styles or adjust to major current events.

Lesson plans are necessary, but a good teacher needs to be flexible, too.

SAMPLE LESSON PLAN THIRD GRADE SCIENCE

Here is what a sample lesson plan might look like:

Buoyancy
Grade Level(s): three
Subject(s): science
Duration: 45 minutes
Description: Students will recognize what makes a clay ball float.
Goals: Experiment with clay to understand what makes something float.

Objectives:

Students will recognize the role of air in flotation.
Students will make changes as necessary to make something float.

Materials: container, water, balls of clay, paper, pencils, pennies
Procedure:
Show the students a ball of clay. Ask them what they think will happen if it's dropped into a bowl of water. Drop it in the water. Ask them why they think it sank. Give each student one ball of clay. Ask them to mold the clay into a shape that will allow their clay to float. Encourage students to be persistent. If time allows, students will add pennies to their "boat," counting how many pennies the boat can hold. As their boat begins to sink again, they continue to change the shape.
Assessment: After the experiment portion of the

lesson, students sketch pictures of which clay shapes sank and which floated and explain why. Discuss as a class: Did weight in the boat influence the buoyancy? How did the shape influence buoyancy? (For example, boats with higher sides kept afloat longer.)
Follow-up: This lesson can continue by using other common materials and testing their buoyancy.

ASSESSMENTS AND COMMUNICATION

Teaching lessons to a class is just part of the process. Teachers need to measure how well the students understand and retain information, as well as how they function in the school setting. Academic work can be evaluated through daily grading of assignments and quizzes. Social development such as respecting people and property is assessed through observation and interaction. Students and their parents see the feedback teachers give when they check student work.

The patterns of reward that a teacher uses to manage a class can provide each student with feedback on his or her behavior. Younger children enjoy seeing a chart with stars after their name, for example. Older students might be asked to participate in assessment and to judge their own progress. A teacher can also use assessments to measure what the class as a whole understands and which concepts continue to be a struggle. As a result, the teacher can tweak upcoming lessons to meet students' needs.

Academic success is more likely when parents, teachers, and students work together as a team.

Ideally, parents and teachers come together for regular conferences during the year. At this time, the regular notes a teacher takes can help paint a larger picture of the child's growth through the school year. Meeting parents can give a teacher better insight into their students' personalities. Teachers can help parents understand how their child manages within the social worlds of school. They can also help parents understand things that are different from when they attended school such as Common Core, IEPs, and additional security measures. If successful, these conferences are a wonderful way for parents and teachers to become partners in challenging, encouraging, and helping a child.

When faculty members work well together everyone benefits.

Teachers share their assessments in a more formal way through report cards and progress reports. Learning how to write these reports in an honest yet polite and helpful way is another important skill that teachers must develop.

WORKING TOGETHER

When teachers work well together, their students benefit. Veteran teachers have hands-on experience. They've encountered many types of parents and students and all sorts of behavior. They've learned how to deal with many different situations. New teachers are familiar with all the latest theories and technology. Experienced teachers and new teachers can learn a lot from one another.

It can be very satisfying when different classes work together. For example, all the classes of the same grade might work together on a joint project. Some schools have also found great success when older and younger students work together, with the older students acting as guides. Older students can read to younger children or teach them how to play chess. In Maryland's Anne Arundel public school system, older and younger students work together in outdoor cleanup projects while learning about their ecosystem. Service projects of this nature can involve every grade. In middle school or high school, incoming students are often paired with members of another class to help them learn the ropes of their new school.

Successful collaboration between classes starts with cooperation among teachers. Working together, they'll develop an idea, plan the parts of the project, and set aside time for students to participate.

TALES OF A TA

Writer Anna Berrigan recalls her time as a college teaching assistant (TA):

"As a student at State University of New York at Purchase, one of my biology professors invited me to be a TA for his lab the following semester. It was a very rewarding experience and a great insight to the impact a dedicated teacher can have.

"Mostly, my job was to hand out and collect materials, answer student questions, and correct quizzes. The first batch of quizzes, the scores were all over the place, as expected. Some students had forgotten there was a quiz and others weren't used to the professor's style. However, by the second quiz, I noticed that one student didn't seem to be grasping the material at all, even though they came to class and did the work.

"The professor and I spoke to the student and realized they had gaps in their reading and test-taking skills. I worked with the student to find simpler texts and visually appealing ways to present the same material. Of course, one semester isn't enough time to overcome large gaps in someone's learning, but because the student came to every lab and participated to the best of their ability, the professor was able to give them a passing grade."

Sometimes a student needs material presented in a different way in order to comprehend the lesson.

CHAPTER FOUR

LEARNING HOW TO TEACH

Schools want to hire the very best teachers—professionals who can connect with students and inspire them to have great careers and be valued community members. Great teachers require certain skills and personality traits, but they also need training. They need to learn how children's minds develop and the best ways to help them learn and grow as people. To achieve this, most prospective teachers must first earn at least one college degree, then a license.

Public school teachers can't teach without a valid teaching certificate, or license, in their state. This license specifies what grades they're qualified to teach. For example, a teaching certificate might state that a person is qualified to teach elementary grades one through six. Teachers in grades seven through twelve need a certificate in secondary education, with an endorsement, or approval, in their subject area. Teaching music requires its own certificate, but this certificate typically can include all grades, kindergarten through grade twelve.

Depending on where they teach, special education teachers might be required to hold a degree in special education, or a major in a content field (such as math) and a minor in special ed. Technical or vocational teachers generally hold a degree and have significant work experience in their field. They undergo additional training before being hired to teach. Private school teachers can often teach without certification if they have a bachelor's degree.

GETTING A TEACHER'S LICENSE

Holding a license ensures that an individual has completed the required coursework and training to be a teacher. To become a licensed teacher, an individual needs to complete courses in teaching and in content areas (arts and sciences). Each state's education department specifies which courses it requires for each certificate. For example, New York breaks down teacher certification by area of interest, subject area, and grade level. So, a candidate who wants to teach middle school science might pursue a license as a classroom teacher, biology, grades seven through twelve.

Teacher trainees also need to practice teaching in a classroom, with supervision, for a certain number of hours. Finally, most states require teachers to pass one or more certification tests before they can get a license. These standardized tests require teachers to show they meet basic standards in reading, writing, math, and other subjects. The exams also test knowledge of the craft of teaching. A background check and/or drug screening might also be required

Most aspiring teachers complete a four-year college program in teacher education that includes the courses needed for certification. For example, to earn an initial license as a classroom teacher for

Prospective teachers need to be passionate and knowledgeable about their subject matter. A certified teaching program shows them the best way to share their knowledge and passion with students.

grades one through six in New York state a candidate needs to complete the following:

- a New York state-registered program: childhood education (grades one through six)
- institutional recommendation: childhood education (grades one through six)
- New York State Teacher Certification Exam: Educating All Students Test (EAS)
- Content Specialty Test (CST): Multi-Subject or Multi-Subject: Teachers of Childhood (Grade 1–Grade 6)
- workshop: Dignity For All Students Act
- fingerprint clearance

Other candidates might pursue teacher education as part of a master's degree program after college. For early education and elementary school, a teacher education program includes courses in specific subjects, such as math and English, and on teaching and learning itself. To prepare students for middle and high school certification, programs focus heavily on the subject the individual wants to teach.

As part of most programs, students need to do one or two student-teaching internships. These generally occur in the last year of college. An internship may last a few weeks or an entire year. A student teacher assists in a real classroom and learns from a head teacher. A teacher education program usually places students in a classroom near the college campus. Each program has a list of cooperating teachers that have agreed (and may be trained) to work with students from the college.

As part of their training, student teachers work in a classroom under the supervision of a more experienced teacher.

Although most internships are unpaid, some colleges allow students to complete student teaching while working at a first job in a school (as an assistant teacher, for example). Students who do this can earn money while completing their requirements. Some programs even allow students to do their student teaching in a foreign country.

SAMPLE CURRICULUM TEACHER EDUCATION PROGRAM

This is a sample curriculum for a master of arts in Curriculum & Teaching offered by Columbia University. Example of a 12-month course of study (full-time)

Fall:
Principles of Teaching & Learning
Critical Perspectives in Elementary Education
Designing Curriculum & Instruction
Integrative Project
Immigration and Curriculum

Spring:
Curriculum Theory and History
Integrative Project
Mathematics in Elementary School
The Teacher: Socio-Historical, Cultural Contexts of Teaching
Gender Difference and Curriculum

Summer:
Disability, Exclusion, and Schooling
School Change
Hip Hop and Cultural Studies in Science Education

Student teachers can use their internships to refine their preferences. For example, someone who wants to be certified to teach elementary school might try two different grades to see if they prefer working with older or younger children. They'll be asked to demonstrate the social skills that make a good teacher which can differ between grades. They should be able to get students to trust them and motivate them to do good work. They should show they are aware of, and sensitive to, students' academic and cultural differences and treat each student with respect. After spending time observing their cooperating teachers, student teachers have the chance to plan and carry out their own lessons with students.

Wherever one enrolls in a teacher education program, it's important to be sure the program is an officially approved one. Organizations such as the National Council for Accreditation of Teacher Education and the Teacher Education Accreditation Council have lists of approved programs. Each state's department of education website should also have lists of approved programs.

KEEPING A TEACHER'S LICENSE

Once a person completes the requirements for a teaching license, they must apply to the department of education in the state where they wish to work. If they attend college in their home state, the school may apply for them. They need to fill out forms, supply proof that they've completed all the requirements and pay application fees. If all the requirements are met, the department officially approves them to teach in that state.

Aspiring teachers should make sure that a teaching program in which they are planning to enroll leads to certification in the state of their choice. Students can be more confident that they will take all the courses needed for certification if they enroll in a state-approved program. Also, students should be sure they will receive a license for the exact class they want to teach, whether it is a grade level or a special subject. The department of education website for the state where the candidate wants to teach should list the requirements for each type of license.

More and more states are giving all new teachers a provisional license. Teachers with this license must work in the classroom for a few years before receiving a permanent license. In New York, licenses are issued in five-year increments. Even a permanent teaching license may not last the length of a teaching career and may need to be renewed. Many states now ask teachers to earn additional credits to renew their license. Many are even requiring teachers to earn a master's degree within the first five years of becoming a teacher.

BOARD CERTIFICATION

Teachers who show additional teaching skill can apply for certification through the National Board for Professional Teaching Standards. This certificate is not required to teach in any state. However, it is recognized by many state departments of education and can simplify the state licensing process.

After working for three years, a teacher can apply for board certification by collecting a portfolio of classroom work and achieving satisfactory scores on four components. Teachers who achieve National Board certification are considered experts in their field. They may be eligible for promotion and a higher salary. There is financial aid available to complete the program. For more information on board certification, contact the National Board for Professional Teaching Standards.

National Board certification consists of four components. The first must be taken at a testing center. The other three may be completed electronically.

OTHER WAYS TO BECOME A TEACHER

The federal No Child Left Behind Act requires that all teachers must be certified. They must be properly trained in educational theories and methodology. Most states offer other ways to become a teacher, especially if one would like to teach in a geographic area or subject that has a teacher shortage. This way of training is called the alternate route. Alternate route programs allow people with college degrees in fields other than education to become certified teachers. Each state offers its own guidelines on how to complete this training.

Those taking an alternate route may begin teaching under a head teacher while they take education courses on the side. Some alternate programs approve people to teach for one or two years before they receive permanent licenses. States that desperately need teachers may give out emergency licenses, which allow people to start teaching right away. During the pandemic, the extreme shortage of teachers meant that substitute teachers who didn't hold a valid license were utilized.

The alternate route is helpful for a person who is older and may be working in another career, but then decides that they want to become a teacher. Individuals who want to teach math and science may find more of these programs, since there is a greater need for these teachers. Also, urban schools that have a shortage of teachers may offer programs such as this. Vocational education teachers may enjoy an alternate route to teaching without a college degree if they have a solid work history and professional certifications in their chosen field. Those who are interested in taking the alternate route can contact school districts or state departments of education for more information.

AN INTERVIEW WITH LINDSEY WOOD, MUSEUM EDUCATOR

What do you think are the benefits of learning in a museum, as opposed to a classroom setting?
"Many museums offer chances to learn with more of the senses that can sometimes be harder in classrooms. You can see actual tools, plants, animals, materials, and even environments up close, hearing the sounds they make, experiencing smells, and sometimes even getting to handle them. A classroom wouldn't be able to fit a real giraffe inside and most schools don't have 18th century wells that you can actually draw water from but going to a zoo or historic site can offer these things."

What kind of degrees or certifications do you hold?
"I first majored in history in college to earn my bachelor's degree. I later became certified in public history and earned a master's degree in museum studies."

What's your favorite part of working in a living history museum?
"I love that I continue to learn by working in a living history museum. Wearing historical clothing helps me teach visitors what people in different time periods dressed like and at the same time I learn why people wore the clothes they did. I notice how my wide-brimmed hat protects me from sunburn and how flowy skirts keep me cool. In order to teach visitors how to do chores and activities people in the past would have I practice using the tools and learn what tricks and strategies work well and get the best results."

What's the most challenging aspect of your career?
"Museum educators often have to be keeping track of a lot of different things at once. People visit museums to learn about the places and things on display, but the museum educator is also responsible for making sure everyone is safe in settings many people are not used to (being close to fires, handling sharp or heavy tools, going up and down steep and narrow staircases, etc.). We are also responsible for protecting the museum objects that are often very old and fragile so that they will still be around for hundreds of years more for people to come and see. Being aware of what everyone is doing when leading a large tour group or teaching multiple people how to do something can be very challenging."

Educators at living history museums such as Colonial Williamsburg demonstrate how people dressed and lived in 18th century America.

CHAPTER FIVE

YOUR FIRST TEACHING JOB

Generally, people who want to teach are good students themselves. They enjoy being in a school and being part of the culture that exists there. They get good grades and participate in school activities. They're high-achieving students who want to help other people excel and reach their goals. Building a good transcript to apply to college is something that starts early in a student's academic career. Aside from concentrating on their current schoolwork, aspiring teachers should be thinking about the future. Would they like to teach young children or teens? Many subjects or specialize in one? Ideally, they should have a good idea of what they want to do when they start applying to colleges.

Even with this decision made, teaching can be a very different experience from school to school and community to community. A teacher training program can help one consider the advantages and disadvantages of teaching in different types of school settings. For example, student teaching placements allow one to experience the day-to-day feel of a school and see if the setting is a good fit.

Another way to gather information is to visit and interview teachers in different places. Whether rural, urban, suburban, private, public, or charter, each school setting brings a unique group of issues. For example, public schools are influenced by state and local politics, which can be frustrating. However, many public school teachers belong to a union which affords them certain protections. It's possible to get a job at a private school without a license, but private schools tend not to be unionized. A religious school might require teachers to attend services, teach religious classes, or even abide by a certain code of conduct in their private lives. That's a lot to consider.

WHERE WOULD YOU LIKE TO WORK?

Schools, even ones in the same town, can be very different from one another. More affluent neighborhoods tend to have cleaner, safer, and better-equipped schools. To "level the playing field," large cities will sometimes assign children to schools in different parts of the city.

To decide where they would like to teach, teaching candidates can ask questions of each school they investigate: What is the school's larger "culture" and vision of teaching? For example, some schools allow students to talk and be boisterous in the hallways, while others require children to walk in silent, orderly rows. A person of deep personal faith might be content teaching in a religious school.

It's good when parents are involved in their child's education and actively support their school.

A teacher will be happiest if their own vision is a good match with the school's.

It is also a good idea to learn more about the school community to understand the needs of the students. Are there many students who speak English as a second language? How many students are in special education programs? Has the community been growing or shrinking in size, and why? How does the school perform on state standardized tests, and will these tests play a large role in the school year? How involved are parents? And how involved are people who aren't parents? What is the teacher turnover rate, or how many teachers are leaving the school each year? For those who have remained, how long have they been teaching there?

Practical questions are also important. If the job requires a move to a new area, what kind of community is it? Also, it's helpful to learn about the pay and benefits that the school offers. Is the pay good for that part of the state or country? What benefits will be provided? Is the school unionized? Would it be possible to get more

There have been many news stories recently involving members of communities trying to impose their own preferences or morality on school libraries and curriculums.

training and become an administrator, curriculum coordinator, or other specialist in the future? Should you decide to become board certified, will the school or district cover some or all of the cost?

INTERVIEWING

Once teaching candidates have completed course requirements and applied for state licensure (or completed the requirements for alternative certification), they are ready to begin interviewing for positions. Today, most job hunts begin online. Schools post teaching jobs on websites such as Indeed, LinkedIn, or local employment sites. A school district's website might list job openings. However, be prepared to be directed to an online recruitment site to apply. Your résumé and supporting documents should be formatted to be uploaded to whatever site the school or district is using.

If a candidate knows someone personally, a friendly call or email might be helpful, but most application paperwork is handled electronically.

If a job hunter wants to expand a search, they may be eligible to teach in a neighboring state, thanks to reciprocity agreements that states offer to those with certification elsewhere. Each state's reciprocity agreements are different, so they need to check the details.

College career counselors have a wealth of information for teachers. They may have information on upcoming teacher job fairs, which may be live or virtual. At a job fair, one can have a mini interview with a school representative and then follow up on available positions. The college employment office may also know of state or county programs that help get new teachers into the classrooms where they are needed.

If a desirable school district has no job openings, a determined person can apply to work as a teacher's aide or substitute teacher in the targeted school district. Substitute teachers are in high demand right now. Being present in the school can help with a job search because principals prefer to hire someone who is already a tested asset to the school.

FIRST-YEAR ADVICE

A teacher's first year is usually the most important. The classroom has a way of shoving theory aside and putting surprise after surprise in front of a new teacher. Seasoned teachers can offer new teachers advice to help guide them through this tricky time. Here are some tips:

- Be very, very prepared. If you are confident, students will feel confident about you.
- Create a short list of class rules about homework, bathroom breaks, etc., to help keep the class focused. For younger grades, parents can sign and return the rules.
- Seek out a more experienced teacher you admire as a mentor. This is the best guarantee that a new teacher will succeed, according to Ellen Moir of University of California, Santa Cruz's New Teacher Center.
- Observe other classrooms to see how other teachers run them.
- Communicate with the school's principal and administrators. Don't be shy.
- Share your love of learning with students.
- Be flexible.
- Keep a sense of humor.
- Find healthy ways to handle stress.

GETTING HIRED

When attending a job fair, meeting school administrators, or interviewing for a teaching position, it's important to already look the part of a teacher. The best bet is to dress neatly and conservatively. Applicants should be neatly groomed and mindful of excessive jewelry or fragrances. Learning about the school ahead of time shows that a candidate is serious about their career and would be a good addition to the staff. At job fairs, job hunters have only about 30 seconds to make an impression, unless the discussion turns into a sit-down interview. Either way, candidates can practice how to "sell" themselves—or sum up unique strengths—so they can share that information clearly and directly when the chance comes.

Once a new teacher is hired, they have a new goal: adjusting to and succeeding in their first classroom.

STARTING YOUR FIRST TEACHING JOB

All new jobs have a learning curve, but new teachers stand in front of a class on Day One and are asked to do the same job as experienced veterans. Instead of having the chance to ease into the profession, beginning teachers are often given the most difficult jobs or classes. New teachers are most in need at schools where more teachers have left, sometimes because of the challenges there or burnout from the pandemic. Also, new teachers must learn to teach their own classes and navigate relationships with parents, administrators, and other teachers at the same time.

How do beginning teachers increase their chances of success? Participating in a mentoring program can make a big difference. A mentoring program provides new teachers with a more experienced "coach" who teaches at a similar grade level. In such a program, new teachers can find an outlet for questions, concerns, and frustrations. The mentor can share general wisdom or suggest practical solutions to classroom challenges. In a small school, the mentor may be able to give guidance on dealing with particular students.

Although business casual is the norm these days, applicants should consider dressing up a bit for their interview.

Stephanie Hansen, a Chicago kindergarten teacher, told *Catalyst Chicago* magazine that her mentor helped her find an alternative to helping 23 students at once.

"I was walking around trying to see what [one] student had written, while keeping [other students] focused on the assignment. And they all wanted my attention."

Her mentor suggested she break the class into small groups that met daily, allowing her to spend time with each child in the group. It worked.

"It is a much more organized workshop, and my students' writing has improved," she reported.

An experienced teacher can help put things in perspective. It can be hard for new teachers to not take things personally, such as an insult from a student or criticism from parents. The first few years as a teacher often require strength and endurance. A mentor can keep a new teacher focused on their success stories instead of the problems.

As studies show how important they are, more and more schools are creating mentoring programs. The state of New York has dedicated funds for a teacher mentorship program for the next five years. The hope is that mentors will help new teachers improve their practical skills and feel supported in their jobs, leading to career stability and longevity. Even if a school doesn't offer a formal mentoring program, a new teacher can still request a mentor.

AN INTERVIEW WITH JAN CZINKE, FORMER EARLY CHILDHOOD SPECIAL EDUCATION TEACHER, TEACHING ASSISTANT AND CURRENTLY A REGISTERED BEHAVIOR TECHNICIAN

You've worked in several capacities with special needs children. What drew you to this field?

"I initially wanted to be an English teacher because I loved English. Watching my teachers deal with some of my classmates made me realize that I really didn't want to teach teenagers. An adult friend watched me work with a group of young girl scouts who were totally unprepared for working on the merit badge that I was covering. She noticed that I was able scrap all of my planning for the day, and quickly change my approach to working with these girls. At the end of the day, they had completed a large part of the merit badge. She mentioned to me that I showed a lot of the skills that special education teachers need and encouraged me to think about that. My guidance counselor at school set up a chance for me to volunteer with special education students and I fell in love with it."

What kind of degrees or certifications do you hold?
"I have a bachelor's degree in special education. (A master's degree is required now.) I formerly had a New York state teaching certificate as a special education teacher. I now have a New York state certificate as a teaching assistant III (level 3). In 2022, I became certified as a registered behavior technician (my current job)."

What's your favorite part of working with special needs kids?
The creativity and inventiveness that I need to use to bring out their full potential.

What's the most challenging aspect of your career?
Dealing with paperwork and government regulations. It takes away a lot of the time that I need to use on planning and inventing new approaches.

Working with special needs kids is challenging, but also immensely rewarding.

CHAPTER SIX

WHAT DOES THE FUTURE HOLD?

Currently, the BLS predicts growth of about 1 percent in the teaching profession over the next decade. Some new jobs will open as today's teachers move into administration or other roles within the school system. Others will become available as teachers grow older and retire. However, teaching is an essential profession with millions of jobs, so 1 percent growth is still thousands of jobs available each year.

WHERE WILL THE JOBS BE?

The number of teachers a school district can hire depends on how much money the town and state have in their budgets. One area that's experiencing growth is early childhood education. These programs are growing because more money is being made available. Studies have found that these early programs help young children get a stronger start. In particular, early childhood programs for special needs children are expanding. This is to fulfill federal laws that state every child is entitled to a free, appropriate public school education.

According to U.S. News and World Reports, many places are experiencing teacher shortages. Although there had been a shortage of staff before 2020, many teachers have resigned or retired due to disruptions and stress caused by the pandemic. To help fill staffing gaps, some schools have offered retired teachers bonuses to return to the classroom. Others have asked staff to work outside their normal scope of duty.

In all states, there are usually more available teaching positions in urban or rural communities than in suburban ones. Inner-city public schools have a harder time keeping new teachers and usually have openings each year. Urban schools especially need teachers with energy and imagination, as they often include students who are living in poverty or who have recently emigrated from other countries. In addition, as more English as a second language (ESL) students enter U.S. schools, schools need bilingual teachers who can teach in both English and Spanish.

Urban and inner city schools can have special challenges, such as gang activity or poverty.

In 2009, the Boston Plan for Excellence found that new city teachers needed help and coaching from experienced teachers to have a good first year. Since then, Boston schools have tried to pair new teachers with a mentor. This program has been used as the model for national mentorship programs. New York state has a similar mentorship program. Those interested in working at an urban school should find out how they support their new teachers through the first few years of teaching.

In rural areas, towns have fewer residents and fewer students in school. The pool of candidates for the available teaching jobs can be thin, since many of the area's young adults may have moved away or pursued other careers. Rural schools usually pay lower salaries than suburban and urban areas, especially if the area has a lower cost of living. But for those who can move to a rural town to teach and would enjoy country life, this can be a good choice.

For a long time, many families viewed Catholic schools as a good alternative to public education. However, rising tuition coupled with declining enrollment has forced many Catholic schools to close.

OTHER TYPES OF SCHOOLS

Families like to have choices about their children's education, especially in areas where the public schools are not strong. Some parents also object to young children being bussed across the city, instead of attending a neighborhood school. Charter schools and private schools are the two largest categories of schools that people choose as alternatives.

A charter school is an experimental public school that is granted a charter by its state to operate independently. Charter schools are given state money to operate, but they don't have to follow the same rules as the other public schools in the area. However, they can't charge tuition, be affiliated with a religion, or require entrance exams. They have the freedom to establish their own missions, goals, and approaches to education. They are smaller, enrolling about half the students of the average public school. Most charter schools have a clear approach to teaching and look for teachers who will follow it. For example, a charter school's approach might include strict behavioral and academic discipline or an environmentally based study of all subjects. To keep its charter, each charter school must show the same strong grades and test scores as public schools.

Interest in charter schools has grown, and many people, especially in urban communities, are pleased that their children have this option. In New Jersey, the highest-performing urban charter schools had higher test scores in 2009 than schools in wealthy, suburban communities. Still, prospective teachers shouldn't expect a huge jump in teaching jobs at charter schools just yet. The success rates

AN INTERVIEW WITH MARGARET PIERCE, ELEMENTARY SCHOOL MUSIC TEACHER

A tragic reality of the 21st century is school shootings. Was this issue discussed at all when you were training to become a teacher?

"I graduated in 2001, so Columbine [a 1999 high school shooting] happened when I was a sophomore in college. I'm sure it was discussed at the time, but we really didn't have a language for talking about it yet. All I remember is thinking that the teaching field was going to change and that it could and probably would happen again."

As the Sandy Hook [2012] and Robb Elementary [2022] school shootings have shown, any level of school is at risk. Would this have affected your decision to choose a teaching career?

"I don't think it would have. Even before school shootings became as commonplace as they are today, there were plenty of people I respected telling me I shouldn't go into this field . . . including some teachers. The pay isn't always great for the level of education you're expected to maintain, it's a high-stress job that you can't help but take home with you, and from time to time we become the targets of parental or community anger. School shootings certainly figure into all of that, but I don't think they would ever be the deciding factor of whether I do this job or don't. Ultimately, there are a lot more reasons that I want to be a teacher."

How does your school or district prepare for an active shooter incident?

"We run lockdown drills, and we have periodic tabletop drills where law enforcement come in and talk to us about best practices. We try to keep the lockdown drills as age appropriate and stress free for kids as possible. We treat them the way that we do fire drills, focusing on the importance of following directions and staying calm and quiet so adults can do their jobs. I think a lot of what teachers do is to walk ourselves mentally through different scenarios. There are three different basic responses in an active shooter situation. They are run, hide, and fight. It's important for someone like me, for whom fighting doesn't come naturally, to at least imagine what that would be like, so that if it ever does happen, we are less likely to freeze. That part is really unpleasant, and sometimes intrudes on my out-of-school life, like when I'm in a grocery store and I start wondering where the nearest exit is, or whether I can accurately tell the direction and distance of certain sounds."

are mixed, and charter schools that show low test scores or another kind of failure can be closed by the state. Charter schools may grow slowly since states can limit the size of these schools. Moreover, these schools receive less state money than public schools. As of 2019, 45 states and Washington, D.C., allow charter schools. However, this doesn't mean they're available in all locations.

Private schools enroll students whose families pay tuition. While teachers in training might imagine themselves working on a large, beautiful campus with stone buildings, most private schools are smaller and found in urban areas. They may be housed in older buildings. They may be religious in orientation—most often Catholic—and may include religious lessons as part of the students' education. Private school teachers aren't required to be licensed. Some teachers find they have more say over how they would like to run their classroom and what they would like to teach. However, these schools do expect that teachers will support the institution's religious goals. They may be required to teach religious education classes and attend services. They may also be expected to comply with a particular code of behavior, even outside of school. Many private schools are able to choose the students they will accept, and so the students may be strong learners.

Overall, the number of students in all grades at private schools has grown smaller since 1990. Because they run on tuition money and donations, private schools can be hit harder by recessions, and private school teachers don't usually have the protection of tenure. Also, private schools typically offer smaller salaries than public schools and may not have the same retirement and health benefits. With smaller staffs, they also may ask teachers to be more involved in extracurricular clubs and teams. Private school teachers are less likely to belong to unions.

However, there are also advantages to teaching at a private school. Some private schools offer teachers discounted housing on the campus. This savings can be a big help for a young teacher. Private schools may also give a new teacher more freedom in the classroom, including more choice in what and how to teach. This can be nice for those who would like to experiment with different approaches and see

The recent COVID-19 pandemic meant that teachers and schools had to figure out new ways to use technology for distance learning.

what works best with their students. Like every other step along their career path, deciding where they'd like to teach requires careful thought and research on the part of teachers.

THE CLASSROOM OF THE FUTURE IS HERE

Technology plays a big part in today's classroom. Some schools have exchanged chalkboards for whiteboards, which can be used for both traditional lessons and computer-based lessons. Many school communications happen via the school's website, automated text messages, or email. Summer reading lists and supply lists are often posted online.

Although most kids use computers daily, typing their homework and doing research on the internet, the pandemic made distance learning the "new normal." Schools and families scrambled to provide laptops to students so they could attend virtual classes at home. Teachers had to master online meeting programs such as Zoom.

Today's classrooms feature sophisticated technology that's used every day.

Unlike the days of separate computer labs, today's computers and other technology are a constant presence in classrooms. Some teachers find that technology helps them reach students who learn differently. Visual and auditory learners, for instance, seem to learn best when they can see and hear a lesson with multiple forms of media. Tactile (hands-on) learners may learn best when they can get out of their chairs and do a presentation or experiment. Using technology to serve different kinds of learners will probably become more common in the future.

PROJECTED GROWTH AREAS FOR TEACHERS

- special needs early education
- preschool/early education
- full-day kindergarten
- mathematics
- science (especially chemistry and physics)
- bilingual education
- foreign languages

Although the past couple of years have proven challenging, there will always be a need for well-trained, enthusiastic teachers. Teaching is a solid career with comfortable pay and benefits. Teachers are valued members of any community. They work in schools, museums, zoos, and even outer space. Most people had a favorite teacher or two who encouraged them to dream big and become better than they thought they could be. Perhaps you might be the one to inspire the next generation of students.

For many teachers, forming connections with their students is the most rewarding part of their job.

10 GREAT QUESTIONS TO ASK A TEACHER

Here are some questions to ask a teacher. Try to talk to teachers in different grades or schools to get different perspectives.

1. What kind of degree did you have when you started teaching?
2. What kind of degree do you have now?
3. How often do you have to take continuing education classes to maintain your license?
4. Are you board certified? Is that something you aspire to?
5. Have you always taught this grade? Why did you choose it?
6. Would you like to be a principal or administrator someday?
7. How many schools have you worked in?
8. Do you belong to a union?
9. What do you think is the most challenging aspect of being a teacher today?
10. Is there anything you wish someone had told you when you first considered this career?

What other questions can you think of?

Everyone has that special teacher they remember—the one who inspired them to be their very best. Maybe someday you can be that teacher to someone!

GLOSSARY

academics: Activities related to learning subjects at a school.

administrator: A person, such as a principal, who oversees a school and supervises its teachers.

alternate route: A way to earn a teaching certificate for those with degrees and experience in other fields.

auditory learner: Someone who learns best by hearing the information, such as in a lecture.

autism: A condition that interferes with a person's ability to communicate and relate to others.

bilingual: Using two languages.

budget: A set amount of money to spend.

burnout: Exhaustion, and even hopelessness, that comes with a long period of overwork and stress. Teachers who suffer from burnout are more likely to leave their jobs.

certification: A license that qualifies someone for a job. A teaching certification allows a person to be hired for a public school teaching job.

charter school: A school founded by a group other than a town's school board, but that is supported by taxes. The school board grants the school a charter to operate independently but is allowed to pull the charter if the school fails to meet certain standards.

curriculum: The classes and academic categories offered in a school.

dyslexia: A learning disability marked by difficulty with reading, writing, and spelling.

early childhood education: The education a child receives in preschools or day care facilities. Early childhood education includes any schooling received before kindergarten.

emergency certification: A rapidly granted teaching certificate for those without traditional teaching qualifications. Emergency certificates are used to solve teacher shortages in high-need areas or teaching categories.

English as a second language (ESL): Refers to an education in which, or a student for whom, English is learned after another native language.

extracurricular: Relating to activities held by a school, usually after the class day is over, such as sports or clubs.

mentor: A wise counselor or guide. In teaching, a mentor is an experienced, or master, teacher who helps guide a beginning teacher.

permanent license: The teaching license earned in the state of one's choice once all requirements have been met. It follows a provisional teacher's license.

provisional license: An initial license granted to beginning teachers. It is not permanent.

reciprocity agreement: An agreement that allows a teacher who is licensed in one state to teach in another. Reciprocity agreements vary by state.

secondary: The level of schooling that includes junior high school and high school, or grades seven to twelve.

standardized test: A test that tries to measure how well large numbers of students in the same grade understand reading, writing, and mathematics concepts.

tenure: A job benefit earned by teachers who have taught at a school for a certain number of years. Tenure protects a teacher from being fired without cause.

turnover: The problem caused when trained, certified teachers quit, leaving a school to hire and train new teachers again and again.

vocational: Related to skills that can be used for a career, such as car repair, cooking, carpentry, or hairstyling.

FOR MORE INFORMATION

AMERICAN FEDERATION OF TEACHERS (AFT)

555 New Jersey Ave NW
Washington, D.C. 20001
(202) 879-4400
Website: www.aft.org
Facebook: @AFTunion
The AFT is a teachers' union that was founded in 1916. It represents more than 1.7 million American teachers.

CANADIAN TEACHERS FEDERATION (CTF)

2490 Don Reid Drive
Ottawa, ON K1H 1E1
Canada
(613) 232-1505
Website: www.ctf-fce.ca
Facebook: @CTF.FCE
Instagram: @ctffce
The CTF is a trade union representing 365,000 elementary and secondary school teachers across Canada.

COUNCIL FOR EXCEPTIONAL CHILDREN (CEC)

3100 Clarendon Blvd
Suite 600
Arlington, VA, 22201-5332
(888) 232-7733
Website: www.exceptionalchildren.org
The CEC is a professional organization for teachers who work with children with special educational needs—those with disabilities as well as those considered gifted.

COUNCIL FOR HIGHER EDUCATION ACCREDITATION (CHEA)

One Dupont Circle NW
Suite 510
Washington, D.C. 20036
(202) 955-6126
Website: www.chea.org
Facebook: @www.chea.org
CHEA advocates for higher education accreditation and quality assurance.

EDCAN NETWORK

60 St. Clair Ave. East
Suite 703
Toronto, ON M4T 1N5
Canada
(416) 591-6300
Website: www.edcan.cea-ace.ca
Facebook: @cea.ace
Instagram: @edcannetwork
The EdCan Network is a professional organization for K-12 teachers in Canada. Its site is available in both English and French.

NATIONAL ASSOCIATION FOR THE EDUCATION OF YOUNG CHILDREN (NAEYC)

1401 H Street NW
Suite 600
Washington, D.C. 20005
(202) 232-8777
Website: www.naeyc.org
Facebook and Instagram: @NAEYC
The NAEYC is a professional organization for members of the early childhood education community.

NATIONAL ART EDUCATION ASSOCIATION (NAEA)

901 Prince Street
Alexandria, VA 22314
(800) 299-8321
Website: www.arteducators.org
The NAEA is a professional organization for art educators who teach pre-K through college.

NATIONAL BOARD FOR PROFESSIONAL TEACHING STANDARDS (NBCT)

1525 Wilson Blvd.
Suite 700
Arlington, VA 22209
(703) 465-2700
Website: www.nbpts.org
The NBCT offers board certification in 16 different teaching disciplines for K through 12 educators in the United States.

NATIONAL CENTER FOR EDUCATION STATISTICS (NCES)

550 12th Street, SW
Washington, D.C. 20202
(202) 403-5551
Website: www.nces.ed.gov
NCES is part of the Institute of Education Sciences, which in turn is part of the U.S. Department of Education. NCES is the federal agency responsible for collecting and analyzing data related to education.

NATIONAL EDUCATION ASSOCIATION (NEA)

1201 16th Street NW
Washington, D.C. 20036-3290
(202) 833-4000
Website: www.nea.org
The NEA is the largest labor union in the United States. It represents nearly 3 million teachers.

NATIONAL SCIENCE TEACHING ASSOCIATION (NSTA)

405 East Laburnum Avenue
Suite 3
Richmond, VA 23222
(703) 524-3646
Website: www.nsta.org
Facebook: @NSTA.FB
Instagram: @official_nsta
The NSTA is a organization for teachers and other professionals in the field of science education.

UNITED FEDERATION OF TEACHERS (UFT)

52 Broadway
New York, NY 10004
(212) 331-6311
Website: www.uft.org
Facebook: @uftny
The UFT is the union that represents most of New York City's public school teachers.

FOR FURTHER READING

Anderson, Mike. *What We Say and How We Say It Matter: Teacher Talk That Improves Student Learning and Behavior*. Alexandria, VA: ASCD, 2019.

Boogren, Tina. *Supporting Beginning Teachers*. Bloomington, IN: Marzano Resources, 2021.

Bush, Lisa. *Teaching Well: How Healthy, Empowered Teachers Lead to Thriving, Successful Classrooms*. Markham, ON, Canada: Pembroke Publishers Limited, 2019.

Emerson, Michelle. F*irst Class Teaching: 10 Lessons You Don't Learn in College*. Hoboken, NJ: Jossey-Bass, 2023.

Endsley, Kezia. *Education Professionals: A Practical Career Guide*. Lanham, MD: Rowman & Littlefield, 2019.

Given-Wilson, Rachel, and Annalise Silivanch. *Your Future as a Teacher*. New York, NY: Rosen Young Adult, 2020.

James, Michael. *A First-Year Teacher's Survival Adventure: A Tale of Lessons Learned*. Independently published, 2023.

Parkay, Forrest W. *Becoming a Teacher 11th Edition*. Hoboken, NJ: Pearson Education, Inc., 2020.

INDEX

N

P

R

S

ABOUT THE AUTHOR

KATHLEEN A. KLATTE is the author of many nonfiction books for children and teens. Topics range from animals and nature to constitutional law to unusual career choices. She lives in New York with one cat and far too many books and Legos.

PHOTO CREDITS

Photo credits: Cover, p. 1 Chris Howey/Shutterstock.com; pp. 1, 3-96 Merydolla/Shutterstock.com; p. 4 Maglara/Shutterstock.com; pp. 5, 22, 46 Monkey Business Images/Shutterstock.com; p. 7 Juliya Shangarey/Shutterstock.com; p. 9 STUDIO MELANGE/Shutterstock.com; p. 11 Queenmoonlite Studio/Shutterstock.com; p. 16 DGLimages/Shutterstock.com; p. 18 Lorena Fernandez/Shutterstock.com; p. 19 plutmaverick/Shutterstock.com; p. 21 Vibe Images/Shutterstock.com; p.25 Krakenimages.com/Shutterstock.com; p. 27 Lopolo/Shutterstock.com; p. 28 smolaw/Shutterstock.com; p. 29 Prostock-studio/Shutterstock.com; p. 32 Shift Drive/Shutterstock.com; p. 34 MalikNalik/Shutterstock.com; p. 35 https://commons.wikimedia.org/wiki/File:Zero-G_training_for_crew_of_1985_and_1986_space_shuttle_missions.jpg; p. 38 Drazen Zigic/Shutterstock.com; p. 39 ESB Professional/Shutterstock.com; p. 41 Ground Picture/Shutterstock.com; p. 43 Indian concepts/Shutterstock.com; p. 47 fizkes/Shutterstock.com; p. 49 Pressmaster/Shutterstock.com; p. 52 Drazen Zigic/Shutterstock.com; p. 53 VH-studio/Shutterstock.com; p. 57 YuRi Photolife/Shutterstock.com; p. 61 Ritu Manoj Jethani/Shutterstock.com; p. 64 Erika J Mitchell/Shutterstock.com; p. 65 Finn stock/Shutterstock.com; p. 69 ASDF_MEDIA/Shutterstock.com; p. 71 Bangkok Click Studio/Shutterstock.com; p. 73 art4stock/Shutterstock.com; p. 74 Cynthia Farmer/Shutterstock.com; p. 79 Travelpixs/Shutterstock.com; p. 80 New Africa/Shutterstock.com; p. 81 Krakenimages.com/Shutterstock.com; p. 83 PeopleImages.com - Yuri A/Shutterstock.com.